After the Ark

After the Ark

Luke Johnson

NΩY Books™

The New York Quarterly Foundation, Inc.
New York, New York

NYQ Books™ is an imprint of The New York Quarterly Foundation, Inc.

The New York Quarterly Foundation, Inc.
P. O. Box 2015
Old Chelsea Station
New York, NY 10113

www.nyqbooks.org

First Edition

Set in New Baskerville

Layout and Design by Raymond P. Hammond
Cover Illustration by Patrick Howard | www.brotherkoala.com

Library of Congress Control Number: 2010934128

ISBN: 978-1-935520-39-9

After the Ark

ACKNOWLEDGMENTS

Many thanks to the editors and readers of the following journals and anthologies in which these poems—some in earlier versions—first appeared or are forthcoming: *32 Poems, 42opus, Beloit Poetry Journal, Birmingham Poetry Review, Brooklyn Review, Crab Orchard Review, Epoch, La Fovea, Georgetown Review, Ghoti, The Greensboro Review, Hollins Critic, The New York Quarterly, Nimrod International Journal, Passages North, Poet Lore, Poetry East, Potomac Review, RATTLE, Roanoke Review, Sou'wester, storySouth, Tar River Poetry, Third Coast,* and *Waccamaw.*

"Poinsettias" appeared in *Best New Poets 2008* and "Remembering the Old Testament While Walking the Dog" appeared in *Best New Poets 2010.*

Thanks to Raymond Hammond and everyone at NYQ Books for their talents and for believing in these poems.

I am forever grateful to my teachers for their encouragement, their editorial guidance, and their fine examples, especially Aaron Baker, Kevin Boyle, Cassandra Kircher, Jeanne Larsen, Thorpe Moeckel, Drew Perry, and Eric Trethewey. I'm also indebted to the careful eyes and insights of Matthew Nienow, Will Schutt, and Keith Montesano. A special debt of gratitude is owed to Cathryn Hankla, for giving me furniture and helping this book find its center.

I'm immensely grateful to my father, Rev. Robert L. Johnson, for teaching me to love language and the way a human voice sounds in an empty church. If not for my parents, their love, their bookcases, and their level-headed pulpits, these poems would never have been written. I'll be thanking them as long as the world will allow me. Thanks, too, again and again, to all my friends and family. This book is dedicated to my mother.

for
Reverend Katie Finney
(1948 - 2002)

CONTENTS

II.

Nor'easter

In white so deep, all lights the same,
the highway buried sky: a grave
of drifts. That morning nothing changed,
in white so deep all lights the same:
my mother's skull cap, bare and plain,
the way she remembered sun and shade.
In white so deep, all lights the same,
the highway buried, sky a grave.

I.

Moving Day

All that was left were the boxes of sermons
collected in her study, thirty years
of readings and reflections, prayers ready
to be gathered and stored away.
I could feel the weight of her words
as I carried the stack of boxes, unsorted,
to my car. With her body of work
tucked into my mid-sized trunk, I returned
for her size-five boots in the crux
of the doorway, dropped them in the backseat.
The breeze stroked the leaves above me,
their rustling like a flock of small birds
taking flight, perhaps frightened
by the muffled click of the trunk's latch.

Laundromat

Waiting for me to finish folding, she
read Southern Living, spun her cane.

If she wanted help she would ask, I supposed,
but I told her anyway out of the goodness

of my guilt,
    Ma'am these dryers are empty,
pointing to the top row. She looked up from her

magazine. I could see the starburst of blue
spider-webbed across her forehead.

She stopped spinning and spoke, *I can't reach
those,* she said, *I've got a problem
       with my equilibrium.*

What I might have said was *Don't we all,*
but instead I nodded, looked at the floor, helped

haul her wet sweat-suits to the dryers, apologizing
for not doing so earlier, whole time thinking

how lucky I was
    that I never saw my mother reach
that age, how she would do laundry downstairs

in the room with the window that looked out
onto my childhood,
      the lake that would freeze

past the docks during winter, and I'd walk
to the brink, lie down on the ice and dip

my hand in the water, feel the cold
on my stomach, flat and solid, but shifting.

Coy-Dogs

If you walked the trees, you'd see cores
strewn through the rows, snatches

of coarse hair marking the highest line
of wire, sometimes a tattered leaf

splotched with blood gusting fallen apples.
Your dog nosed wind and your father watched,

each catching the scent of something wild
as if they knew to expect this new danger:

those twilit woods where your mother
would take you for picnics, supper laid down

beyond fence edges where, timid and mangy,
half-breeds stalked crumbs, hovering out of view.

After frost, their ribcages showed through.
Weeks later, when snow settled mornings

and the woodstove smoked nights, you saw
paw-prints circling the property, here or there

a flattened patch of snow. Run your hand
over the barbs. Test the tautness of the line.

Charged

"In this year terrible signs were seen in the skies over Northumberland, and people were horribly afraid. There was incredible lightning, and fierce winds, and fierce dragons could be seen flying through the air."
—from the *Anglo-Saxon Chronicle*, 793 A.D.

You see them hanging from power lines.
Like tennis shoes. Fruit bats that land
on conductors, perhaps in search
of a blossom, throwing the entire grid
into short circuit. They almost look natural,
leathery wings draped over charred upside-down
torso, skull still steaming. Mummified on the wires,
the crisp thin skin and matted black fur
burns your nostrils while lights flicker house
to house, the air a whisper smoking
through basements and attics like a cloud
in the night sky, invisible except
to the part of you that starts when the power
goes out, stands and walks to the window
as though Death is going to be on
the stoop, cold bone crowned in shadow,
robe flitting while the wind claps its wings.

Deathbed, Imagining Delivery

The doctor and my father spoke of civil
disobedience, while she, nauseous,
begged something to take the edge off,
some balm in liquid Demerol.

Thirsty then, she couldn't drink,
but chewed ice-chips
from a Styrofoam cup. My father walked hallways
for refills, crushing ice to teeth-marks
bitten into the cup's-brim.
                                    We take our turns

waiting, knowing what's ahead.
            It's not shimmering light,
not oft-emptied bedpans, but the rawness
of my father's prayers, that reveals

what I had forgotten: Psalms. The Valley.
Memory casts shadows over malice.
She's out. The past reconciles itself
to itself.

        Here are my sleepless nights:

hymns we would not sing Sundays,
but now read her mornings, voices low;
the IV needle-marks dimpling her palms;
my father's mouth after Amen, the same lips
that once twisted *dyke* at her same body, now failing.

Sunflower and Bird

Too many suns in this watercolor,
each one chasing light across the horizon,
too bright to be candles, too large to be stars.
The bird's eyes, motionless, track every sun.

Often I'll walk past its perch
in the front hallway and see only a flower,
not the beak and wings hidden beneath
a petaled face turning to follow sky.

My mother spent one Christmas away.
She left my brother and me for the family
of the woman she loved, the woman
we saw, knew, struggled to place.

We suffer from over-abundance
of light, how ill-equipped to see—
knowing the danger of staring into the sun—
the way the glass pane can erase

glare, flood our empty hall with daylight
when the door throws wide, showing us
what we always knew was there:
this buried bird, this sunflower, this face.

Crossing

Our lives are labeled with magic
marker, my mother's script on the boxes
in my father's attic, a calligraphy

of what was gone in the way she crossed
her z's and sevens. Willow catkins still sweep
the lawn of our old yard, while none

of us are there enough to see them.
The boxes get jostled every year
when we search for Christmas decorations

or an old photo, the contents rearranged
and shoved back into the corner, covered.
He fell in love again, with the idea of her,

while I fell into her hand, the ink
horizon that I scratch through zed,
a striking dash that weds her and him

and me in our separateness, an ornament
that I hang on to the end of things.

Pageant, Christmas Eve

Full pews lined with burning beeswax.
I was a shepherd boy tending a toddler flock.
My mother, vigilant in her pulpit, told the story
of angels. She opened her eyes wide
for *Hosanna the highest*, shut them
to smile out *peace*. She was the voice
of Gabriel, the same voice I overheard
telling my father she was going to leave.
It sounded distant then, like the plunk
and hiss of lit votives falling in a tub,
like underwater smoke. After the last hymn,
my father and I stayed up past midnight
to light new candle ornaments on our tree.
Houselights snuffed, the dark became an empty
ribcage, the tree our flickering heart.

Appalachian Woodrat

"And first he will see shadows best."
—from Plato's *Republic, Book VII*

Watch for traps in Devil's Marbleyard—
gauntlets of metal boxes laid down
between boulders to snare you
for study, endangered as you've become.

Hawks kettle the sky, wheel.
Maybe you already see the trapdoors
hidden in lichen-covered talus
under granite slabs, giant headstones.

Do you know who's looking for you,
huddled there under rattlesnakeroot
listening to rain soften the moss?
Are you hiding, rock-mouse?

You've learned as prey, forepaws
tending acorns in galleries of shadow,
brown fur thinning in gusts
across the boulder field. In the colonnade

of darkness, you shiver, nose galvanized
air holes. With only one thin coat,
you're bound to freeze in this cave within
caves that once seemed so safe.

Lobster

At hospice, a statue of a heron perched
among cattails, looking fragile in black water,

remaining firm—my mother's body
the antithesis, how it bruised

where my brother gripped her
while she talked about lobster all week:

the ceremony, the satisfaction of parting
meat from shell, the decadent drip-down

of butter finding cracks, pooling in claw-tips.
I sat living with that pond—bulldozed body

filled and stocked with smallmouths—and
the wretched metal bird refusing to unfold.

Glass Doors

If it wasn't for the windows, it would all be so different.
The light forced to choose sides, shadows grow different.

A house of glass with wooden gaps wrapped by trees,
gray inside when it rains, at dawn no different.

Porches hold what's too nice for closets. Reminders.
Rackets and bats, balls you're taught to throw different.

Each new day in a routine trains the eyes, renders
the new old. Teaches what you already know: difference.

Only glass doors can close and remain open, silhouette
the familiar in strange light, how the same can show different.

I remember watching a rabid fox maul a broken boombox
on our old porch, how we moved then: slow, different.

The Heart, Like a Bocce Ball

The jack sits low in the grass. We're dead drunk,
cannonballing across the lawn, gouging
handful divots, each of us still nursing
a tumbler of scotch brought home from the wake.
We sons and brothers and cousins. I spin
my ice and let that black-tie loosening
buzz swarm. The others choose the sky, looping
pop-flies that swirl with backspin, an earthen
thud answering grunts while the soft dirt caves.
I bowl instead, slow-ride hidden ridges—
the swells buried beneath the grass—carving
a curve, a line from start to stop, finish.
The heart, like a bocce ball, is fist-sized
and firm; ours clunk together, then divide.

Poinsettias

Head bowed in the impossible-
posture pews at my mother's church,
I'd close my eyes and call out
the creeds and catechisms of her life,
those prayers like one of her mother's

recipes, steaming on the table
from memory. It's not much different
now, the few times I make it to service,
even when I see in the bulletin
that one of the multitude

of poinsettias at front chapel
is watered in memory of my mother.
I'm probably calling on something
of that childhood, some sense
that I belong where I am,

that it's not just another gallon of gas.
Magnolias bloom at the bottom
of stained glass windows,
and I can hear the prayers of the people,
the inconsequential murmurs

and well-articulated deaths
that the rafters swallow up
until they all sound the same,
like a memory of a time before
memories, of fresh-cut grass and supper.

Tools

My father owns three ball-peen hammers
I've never seen him use, a crosscut saw
we dulled taking down a half-dead oak.

He has a sickle we passed back
and forth to clear nettles and tall grass
when we plotted our white-washed shed

built to hold more tools, where we keep
the bolt-cutters he used to hack
through the holly bushes, to get under

the porch where our old dog crawled.
The mangled hollies didn't survive winter.
Lined up along the shed wall you can see

the rusted machinery we need even
when we don't: rake, shovel. We clear
a corner for a pruner picked from a yard sale.

Every year the shed seems smaller, closer
to the brim. We keep accumulating,
stacking what we find on what we forget.

Apartment Birds

℗

I've learned to let these vanishings go—
towhees flitting from gutter to hedge,

a distant cousin succumbing,
             slick roads and old
not-quite friends hitting telephone poles,

secondhand tragedies
             like losing memories of birds—
the guilt of wanting
             to admit you already forgot.

You would rather these birds stay hidden.

℗

I can muster something better, some reflection
or hologram of grief.
             In one story, told over

a gas pump, the dead swerved
             to miss a cat,
flipped and struck stone culvert, died in a field.

They told me the cat died too and I wondered why.

∛

Out walking I'm almost offended
when something startles me,
                          brash starlings
or grackles devouring
                  a stream of evening lamplight,
the sound of sparrows—

I still jump at these sudden uncoverings,

find a measure of my own wildness
in scaring them
                  as they've scared me.

I give chase. I shout them back to the trees.

Highway Dogs

The first one was snug
against the rumble-strip, loose
tongue hanging dry on the highway,
guts spilled out into morning.

A day later, the same mountain
parkway served up another,
a husky mutt speckled black
with road grime and rubber.

It was then, looking into the woods,
that I could see their playground:
packs of maples and yews licking
at the creek bed, the wooden shade

that crawled under leaves to sleep.
Until a wind gust would furl
a moldy merry-go-round, red
and orange hemlock needles, oak leaves

pirouetting through the trees
and shadows before starting
their see-saw drift back down.
I knew they weren't always dead,

those dogs, that they must have once
been road tramps throwing away
empty barks like prayers.
Something of the road brought them back

from the broken branches,
the trees and the leaves and that cool,
something of the road
and the feel of sun hitting pavement.

Vestigial

It looked like something had taken a bite out of him.
The jagged appendix scar on my father's stomach
pearled with sweat while we worked in the yard,
shaking out mulch bags and pulling weeds.
I knew the story as he told it: during the war
you had to be a soldier to get a real surgeon.

Draped in white, noosed by gray stubble, purple stole.
Had he not been my father, I might have thought
he looked like God. But it wasn't a miracle
he lived; only a med student who learned
to hold a blade from gutting lake trout,
dumb enough to fish into my father's belly.

Down there in the dirt, my father said
there weren't any miracles, only coming in
and going out. We laid down the last sack
of fertilizer and walked over to the porch
where we blew out dandelions like candles,
watching seeds drift like frozen breath, that shine.

Remembering the Old Testament While Walking the Dog

Cobwebs pearl on the hedge-top while the dog
leans on the roots. This part of morning it's just us
and the old-timers taking our walks, a light frost

still dusting the shadowed half of the yard,
sunlight brimming over roofs newly shingled
since the windstorm last month brought down

a live powerline into a pile of leaves,
whipping up a wildfire. Then, the whole valley
smelled like a woodstove during a white winter,

smoke drifting for the sky like morning fog
lifting—What does it mean to be holy, to be
in one place thinking of another, to hear a voice

come from something burning, something alive
fizzling away?—one of those mornings, the only sound
came from a woodpecker hammering an oak tree.

I stood still, listening, straining to hear the fire.

Late Spring

Often at night she'd haunt the porch
to watch the fireflies find the dark.
As though the stars could build a church,
often those nights she'd haunt the porch
and light a citronella torch.
The bugs would flock to flicker, stark.
Often at night she'd haunt the porch,
to watch the fireflies, to find the dark.

II.

Survey Photograph

Icicles teeth eaves. The chimney rages.
It must've been late winter, when curb-snow
sludged brown and the easy smell of woodstoves—
lost along with all the smaller changes—
followed cold wind through the willow catkins,
leaves moving like whitecaps seen from distance.
The fire-pit glows white with garbage ashes
or snow. Our birchwood-pile, dwindling, glistens.

How much we burned there: between attic junk
and rotten lumber, my mother's letters
twined in piles, dated. I watched her script curl
in blue heat, flames catching the basement dank.
There are no ashes to stamp out here, just
old drifts melting to cinders and sawdust.

The View from Faulkner's Balcony, Pirates' Alley

Nuns looked for converts outside the convent.
Anderson and Faulkner, armed with pellet
guns and bourbon, trained bull's-eyes on sisters
ministering. Crosshatch, trigger. Each shot
bounced to the ground off of the thick habits.
They took patient aim, easing pen-blistered
fingers across the muzzles and pulling.
BB's the size of rosary beads, pills.

My mother's nightstand had a place for pills
(lithium bottles, a congregation
of her illness stacked against worn hymnals)
my father would hide. He drank Sauvignon
Blanc on Sundays, cursed nights after preaching.
At baptisms, I watched his hands: pale, reaching.

Vulture Tree

We were never so holy, and apples
in the ministers' orchard rot the same.
Back grove and the black birds drying their wings:
my brother and I hurling cores, flinging
all we could find at them: pocked crabapples,
pinecones, rocks. We'd step away to test our range.
If we ever came close, they might unroost
and rustle branches, letting the loose fruit

fall. Early spring, the tree kept on dying:
knobs, like tumors, jutting from the crotches,
the bark bitten and peeled from our attacks.
And the tree's skeleton sank, the grey sky
seeming heavier. The birds still watched us:
dependable and certain, steadfast-black.

Elm Tree, Hammock, My Mother, Grace

I asked her if I could see the new scar,
a hysterectomy nearly two weeks
faded, and might have known she was too weak
to say no, that I had gone much too far
with her to not already know these curves:
staples winding across her stomach, her
distended belly and bald head, her hands
still strong, rocking us, curled in bands of rope.

And then she lifts her shirt for me. The world
is humming: wasps come down from hidden nests,
a Cessna crop-dusts nearby fields, and motes
of dust will clutch anything. A squirrel,
caught between trees on a too-thin branch, tests
what can hold. Still, above the ground, we float.

Flood

Row-boats paddle Main and leaf-clogged gutters
run over, floating half-filled bird-feeders
off branches. A woman on her roof strips
down. Almost furtive the way she's waving:
covering her chest with one arm, flailing mist
with the other. This lull, while the warped eaves
dry, water keeps rising, the ground softens.
Miles off, couples mute the news and listen:

It's not so hard to imagine the rain.
I long to hear that gallop on tin roofs,
my uncle's—mother's youngest brother—thin
shack where we drained a flask of hundred-proof
scotch after the last ceremony. Stilled,
we put her shoes outside and watched them fill.

Box Kite

Hold on. Adjust to the south gusting wind
by turning your back. Let the thunder clouds
flash off the coast, the air sparking and now
and then a lull, when the kite dips and bends
back toward you, string loosening in your hand.
A breeze is never finished, but will blow
between gales until it seems the waves slow
and the shore moves, sky tied to the sand.

Widows' Walk

The man may never again fix the rocker
lilting back and forth on paint-peeled porch boards
two blocks from the shore, but he'll call out birds
gliding past: *pelican, cormorant, hawk,*
as if hearing their names might stop them.
He knows this long wind, how it can carry
a cold breath or sound out beyond the brim.
Empty, the rain-beaten chair looks stable.

It all has been broken before, clearly
faded planks on the landing and cable
hanging slack off the deck, but our man lives
for a hammer in his hand, salt on skin.
On his roof-top, he's waiting for the waves
to move out, the beach's constant beginning.

Hiking Apple Orchard Falls, After Root Canal

How melting snow draws a map of the shade.
A line in a notebook she gave me, penned
between steps we took across the creek bend
where water gurgled under frozen sheets:
thaw. At least the sound of it, some tune
for walkers working their way to the end,
another frost on its way, but by then
we'll have already left, knowing the view.

There, above the rock face's icy beard,
she asked me about my tooth, if it hurt.
The dentist told me he needed to clear
pulp for re-growth: a throb, a distant stir.
Creek-side, with her, I listened for some dulcet
letting loose: eddies under ice, slow pulse.

Second-Story Window of a Three-Story House

If my breath always failed to fog the glass,
it would tell you something about warmth
and my weakness. If I told the truth
each time you asked about what passed,
you would still doubt me: if I really glanced
through a small window, watching her, smoothing
away her ailing frame. What would you say, you,
if I said I was redrawing a map?

Here, in the middle, we have a choice.
We can hear the water-heater drumming
in the attic or slow footsteps pacing rooms.
Whatever you're waiting for: a voice
you trust yelling these empty stairwells,
echoing, our stories begging a second tell.

Clouds

I'm tired of searching for a meaning
in the things I only half-understand:
a cloud wall casting shadows on the face
of the mountains, why I take down pictures
when I lose someone, the constant greening
of distant foothills. Some reprieve from land
to stare at sky, believing the lacing
cirrus can be something else, can flicker.

Storms and the still hovering light all edge
from one forgotten town toward another.
Watch the blinkered sunset, clouds ablaze
with orange seeping through the sky's fringes.
Maybe they're worth all this mulling over,
the way they linger even as they fade.

Independence Day

The fireworks bloomed across the lake,
exploring the sky, open, distant.
We spread the blanket, pulled it straight
as fireworks bloomed across the lake.
Much more than us, she just gaped
and clapped, so rapt in that bright instant:
the fireworks blooming across the lake,
exploring the sky, open and distant.

III.

Inventory

Frayed cords of rope separate.
I twist them together, knot
the end and recoil, drawing
between hand and elbow
as though this fix could hold.
Old rope too worn to be useful,
too useful to be thrown away.
And the afternoon boils.
Heat dries us out, my father
and I, as we sift through
the shed we're leaving and decide
what's worth keeping. The dog
chases a car down the hill,
returns panting. We sweat.
The sky remains in the sky.
I pick up something, baseball bat
or shovel, toss it into a pile.
But first, I let the heft of whatever
it chooses to be sag in my hands—
bat that drew a thumb-sized welt
over my eye, shovel that halved
a milksnake we thought rattler.

Morgan Opera House

It wasn't what it claimed to be, the stage
was used, but no diva ever saw it, no aria
reverberated through the second story
windows, floated into the village and hung
high notes over the post-office. Overalls, not ties,
were worn to shows, usually comedies.

The village had its own brand of comedy
played out in the library underneath the stage.
I'd find myself there after walking railroad ties
by the lake, where I'd listen to the easy arias
of white caps sloshing onto stones hung
on shore. I could bury my head in a story

in the back book-stacks, overhear stories
of Village Council Members, their dark comedies
kept in closets: the Mayor, who it was heard, hung
dresses in his; or maybe the Deacon who staged
a fight with his wife, so no one would know he loved arias
and a man. I watched them come and go, hypnotized

by how easy they would pat your neck, only to tie
a noose. Not even in my dog-eared stories
could I find such cuddly villains, lambent luminarias
waiting to set the whole village ablaze, a comedy
on wheels pulled by the Wells-Fargo stagecoach
down Main Street. On the library wall there hung

a letter from Mrs. Morgan, whose daughter Jane hanged
herself in a dormitory with a knot she retied
twice before it held taut. I'd seen Jane on stage
upstairs, playing the lead in *West Side Story*.
She sang like the vinyl in the library stacks, a comedy
to compare her to the cast, a real downtown Maria

with a New York City body, torturing boys, sending arias
of want cascading through my head: her naked body hung
onto my leg, or elsewhere. My fantasy a comedy
then, until I heard years later how she cut her ties
with the village. I had rewritten my love story
by then, the one where I showed her books under the stage.

But the books could have told her: the world's a stage
tied to tragedy, without arias or audience, and some comedies
hang on without a joke until you realize it's just another story.

Leaving Cádiz

We stumbled from *una cerveza* to *otra*,
la playa where our tents were hidden
in ruins of a fort. It's enough to start with words

and wait. I kept a pocketknife we used
to shred bars of hash, rolling sticky black
with tobacco spilled from loose cigarettes.

Passing and forgetting, we smoked
like Americans. Our last night, it rained
and I waited to move, sky holding me still.

A classmate had jumped off a bridge
into a shallow gorge, body choking rocks
at lake's mouth. I asked my brother

if he could lose himself to black sky,
leaving crumbling fortress walls and stars
covered by clouds, the feel of a woman's wrist,

if everything could be made less, *nada.*
We watched the surf move out, the beach
its own world, its own weight, and I knew the sun

would rise before I was ready,
but I couldn't let go of that steady rain,
unimportant for hours, moving wet sand

with my fingertips, learning the thinness
of the grain, how small frictions
seemed larger, how easily the night was lost.

Manse

It might be easier to blame the dead
for disrepair: rusty mower blades
in the garage, creaking porch swing
we never thought to fix, ripped tarps.

When my brother calls, it's not
for money anymore, but advice
on distance and crossing it, a girl
I've never met he claims to love.

An old oak tree once came down
in our backyard, trunk stretching
from lake-bank to back-porch,
and the black mark on the bark

made us assume lightning, though
we never heard a storm. We collected
uncapped acorns, planted them in pockets
of muck where creek met lake,

knowing they'd never grow.
He says he's looking for work.
I tell him to take a class. More,
I let it go to the machine.

He spoke at the funeral and I hated him,
not for what he said, but because
I sat rooted and mute. After, we stood
at opposite ends of the same line.

Processional

Hearses like limousines,
which they are, stream
down Highway 58.

Some cars masquerade
as mourners, hop in line
blinkers-flashing to climb

down the mountain, clear-cut
red clay shining ruts
beside the road. So much

that was once so rich
is turning red, these woods
without trees, opossum blood

drying on the road shoulder,
dressed up faces older
than the body we're all

following—the stop and stall
of questions we're afraid to ask:
how long until it's okay to pass?

The clutch floats. I'm neutral
remembering funerals
my father would take me to,

where I'd seek refuge
with the caterers while
he stood robed in the aisle.

So death leads me to stilted
hot plates, heat lamps tilted,
the light showering, the steam

rising, uneven lines and the gleam
of one thing leading to another:
someone's aunt, cousin, mother.

Ex Libris

Before she left, my father would play
Wynton Marsalis and tell us brass

was purer than voice ever could be.
She blared Joplin in the next room.

Behind glass, his first edition of Faulkner's
A Green Bough leaned on her Piercy,

each coming out only after the music
when they sat on opposite sides

of the study. She scribbled marginalia
and his fingers traced the cover, illuminated,

an etching Faulkner picked from a pile:
a naked man and a naked woman both

hiding their faces; he's Atlas shouldering
her world, she's crying into her hands.

In the hallway, I listened for voices, heard
only their pages turning faster and faster.

Demolition

I took down the old wall, hauling wheelbarrows
of mildewed rubble to the dumpster in back,
my mother watching from Linda's window.

I hucked drywall debris to the metal edge,
paused and listened to the racket
clatter back, a cacophony of broken nails,

boards slapping against evening stillness.
That summer still flickers—how I could work
any blade under those floorboards,

sweat and pry at rotting wood, not thinking
about closed bedroom doors, but only
ripping some house apart, fitting tongue to groove.

Evenings I swam to our sailboat, sloop anchored
to orange buoy. My arms burned as though
they were somebody else's. I watched the sky ripple

across lake-glass. I leaned into the boom,
letting the light fade, forgetting the horizon.

Joyful Night

He feeds upon her face both day and night,
And she with true kind eyes looks back on him,
Fair as the moon, and joyful as the light
                                    —Christina Rossetti

A setting summer sun in Clam Gulch
looks like afternoon anywhere else,
the tide out and two monolithic erratics
left dry to wade the shallows, only
to be swallowed by morning.
On a cloudless and ebbing midnight,
a pup-tent pitched beneath sandstone cliff-face,
the campers carve initials held by hearts
and giant rocks stay impossible.
Campfire burns weak, driftwood popping sparks,
sun still lurking under the horizon,
tracing volcanoes, paling sky and scarp.
This night could not belong only to the moon
or sun, but to some current boiling between,
a certain dream, the impulse to head north—
the gleam that flashes fishermans' bar-tops
when a mug slides down—with the stampede speed
of a false-charging Grizzly full gallop.
But this night doesn't seem so fast,
meandering as if it's never been
the place its going, an ornate sentence misread
dawning on its own meaning.
Clouds drag the sky like brushstrokes
or smoke rushing to deliver the night.
A heron glides the contours of shore,
searching the inlet for some stray glint
to rise to the churning surface, some star.

Kachemak Bay Water Taxi

These nights of gunmetal daylight,
I feel drowning in my sleep,
the whirring mosquitoes tiny swells

rising against my tent's nylon hull.
What meanest thou, O sleeper,
O gringo dreaming of the sea?

People remember the story of Jonah,
but forget Nineveh, the utter end
of a place after that great fish's ribs,

Nineveh, where Jonah went to preach,
where he went and asked God
to die, cursing gourds and sackcloths.

We are not cattle, he seemed to say.
The driver calls walruses sea-cows.
I look for them off the bow and see

only killers swimming underneath.
Glaciers tongue horizon. Icebergs turn.
Cormorants stretch their necks.

I duck into the cabin, ask
for another lap around Gull Rock,
floating a bill into the tip jar, squinting

through windows thick with fingerprints.

Hospice Tape #3

Miracles of technology throttle me
less than they do my father, who wept
to see my mother, two weeks dead,

on the camcorder flip-screen,
the flickering stamp of her gaunt face.
She spoke about God and absence,

looking for one in the other,
learning to love my father
only after she had left.

Someone told me an adult life
does not begin until you see a parent die
and know it's possible.

Needle-draws and hospital gowns,
liquid pixels and high-definition,
always light, this aperture for grief.

I rewound to where I was a child,
paused. My father left for his study,
those quiet offices fathers keep.

Apartment Lullaby

Lying in bed, you can hear
the sounds if you just crack
the window—wind chimes
on the neighbor's balcony,
late night drivers susurring
over rain-slick streets,
downspouts slapping
against vinyl siding, gusts
that swirl between whistles
and lean the venetian blinds
inside, the metallic hum
of the AC thrumming on—
it's the wind blowing the world
through the window gap.
The dog is already breathing sleep.
Every so often he'll paw
and whimper in his dream.
Outside, in the yard, another
midnight passes in and out
of the lamplight, bulb
management has replaced
again after someone shattered it,
this time with a golf ball,
that simmering yellow bull's-eye
in the sky, nearby stars
blotted by its 100 watt halo.

Retiring the Night, the Season

It's not the light sparking
as the sun drips down, not
leaves and needles spiraling

to red clay through late afternoon
a too-cold day in October;
it's not these things I'm guilty

of making more than they are.
Extremes trick us into breathing
meaning into empty or at least

half-full gestures, into skin
feeling like skin feels, or trees
behaving how trees ought:

birches bending to break during
an ice snap, roots finding water.
The last time I visited my father,

I sat on his patio in front
of a Dutch oven, told him
I'd split what wood he had,

would stay to make knots
of newspaper, kindling something
warm for us to gather around.

Later: fire and silence, the realization
there was nothing to say.
These flames must run their course.

We poked the smolder, let each
of our insufficient breaths
stoke whatever fire was left to burn.

A Pysanka for My Mother's Poetry Book

It kept the table steady, her marbled
notebook filled with poems.
The pages go blank a few months
after I was born, when the uneven
dining room table needed righting.
There, I watched her hold
her kistka over the candle, letting
it melt words I could not then comprehend
onto the egg surface. She would tell me

what the written-wax meant: why it was
called a pysanka, from the Ukranian *pysaty*
meaning 'to write', she said, and then
translate the symbols, the art.
But I wasn't listening, too captured
by the dyeing process—lowering eggs
into Mason jars full of candlelight.
I watched the oval shadows descend
into wombs of color that would leave their stain.
She used a wooden spoon to scoop
the eggs without cracking them,
the curved wood of its half-bottom
taking every one of my mother's
shades until it was black, just
glistened as it came out the jar mouth.

Corn Snake as Compass

Miles inland, a shrimp boat gathers grass,
rice paddy and swamp swallowing hollow keel.
Dual-masts rise slant, pointing skyward.

Overgrown and out of place. Direction loses
itself at an empty till. Aft and fore become
back and front while the windswept bog hums

with late night traffic. Disembodied headlights
flicker through marsh grass like lanterns.
A corn snake, shedding, uncoils in the hull.

Low gusts blow swelter across the bow, bending
rotten planks, and eventually something snaps.
Then, in that percussive moment beyond summer,

maybe before the boat's skeleton is picked raw,
when no one will hear the fixed rudder rattling,
our snake might move on, trawl the tall stuff

away from this forgotten wood sinking, this shell.

After the Ark

Standing under redwoods, it's easy for me to believe
in giants, to grieve a field of grasshoppers still alive

in wind feathering ferns, ghosts greening
the catkins'-sway.
                              Or maybe my grief changes colors

in memories and books, showing red
as green, a trick of light to cast shimmers

as false shadow.
                              Praying mantes must have ascended
Noah's gangplanks, one male and female, she

resolute in her purpose, he in his expendability.
Such precision cannot be called love.

Hoof-prints reveal the herd where dust kicked
and has resettled.
                              We are not so fallen

that we can't recognize our shadowed edges.
Trees will show their rings without protest

and the ocean sings a chorus of *I do's*, taking in
late-evening quiet along with scores of sinners

still wandering, who come to the coast nights,
who would've drowned in what my mother showed me

of God's love, the ever-lasting compassion
                                        too definite
to be human, but I will hide these small things:

inventions and embellishments on playing fields
I never took, how I lie—even here, even now—how

my mother left my father and I still don't know
how to forgive her, if I need to—Genesis

misses these unpaid fares, and I can only listen
to black water buck while cliffs swallow wind

and spit back memory, pushing clouds to sea.
Belief easier said than done when considering scale,

this is what a cracked shell tells us about growth.
Once the sky has been covered, roots can only drink.

It's up to us to grow gills, to learn to breathe
here where the flood has become the body.

About the Author

Luke Johnson's poems have appeared in *The New York Quarterly, Beloit Poetry Journal, Greensboro Review, Best New Poets,* and elsewhere. His awards include prizes from the Academy of American Poets and the *Atlantic Monthly,* as well as a Tennessee Williams Scholarship from the Sewanee Writers' Conference. He received his B.A. from Elon University and his M.F.A. from Hollins University, where he was a teaching fellow. He lives in Seattle, Washington.

About NYQ Books™

NYQ Books™ was established in 2009 as an imprint of The New York Quarterly Foundation, Inc. Its mission is to augment the New York Quarterly poetry magazine by providing an additional venue for poets already published in the magazine. A lifelong dream of NYQ's founding editor, William Packard, NYQ Books™ has been made possible by both growing foundation support and new technology that was not available during William Packard's lifetime. We are proud to present these books to you and hope that you will continue to support The New York Quarterly Foundation, Inc. and our poets and that you will enjoy these other titles from NYQ Books™:

Barbara Blatner	*The Still Position*
Amanda J. Bradley	*Hints and Allegations*
rd coleman	*beach tracks*
Joanna Crispi	*Soldier in the Grass*
Ira Joe Fisher	*Songs from an Earlier Century*
Sanford Fraser	*Tourist*
Tony Gloeggler	*The Last Lie*
Ted Jonathan	*Bones & Jokes*
Richard Kostelanetz	*Recircuits*
Iris Lee	*Urban Bird Life*
Kevin Pilkington	*In the Eyes of a Dog*
Jim Reese	*ghost on 3rd*
F. D. Reeve	*The Puzzle Master and Other Poems*
Jackie Sheeler	*Earthquake Came to Harlem*
Jayne Lyn Stahl	*Riding with Destiny*
Shelley Stenhouse	*Impunity*
Tim Suermondt	*Just Beautiful*
Douglas Treem	*Everything so Seriously*
Oren Wagner	*Voluptuous Gloom*
Joe Weil	*The Plumber's Apprentice*
Pui Ying Wong	*Yellow Plum Season*
Fred Yannantuono	*A Boilermaker for the Lady*
Grace Zabriskie	*Poems*

Please visit our website for these and other titles:

www.nyqbooks.org